the Weekend Crafter®

Paper Crafting

the Weekend Crafter®

Paper Crafting

20 Projects to Fold, Cut, Mold, Weave & Pierce

TERRY TAYLOR

LARK BOOKS

A Division of Sterling Publishing Co., Inc.
New York

ART DIRECTOR & PRODUCTION:
KATHLEEN HOLMES

PHOTOGRAPHY:
EVAN BRACKEN

ASSISTANT EDITOR:
HEATHER SMITH

ILLUSTRATIONS:
ORRIN LUNDGREN

PRODUCTION ASSISTANCE:
SHANNON YOKLEY

By the author, *To Mother*, 1959. 6 x 9 inches (15.2 x 22.9 cm). Construction papers and crayon. Photo by Evan Bracken.

Library of Congress Cataloging-in-Publication Data

Taylor, Terry, 1952-
    Paper crafting : 20 projects to fold, cut, mold, weave & pierce / Terry Taylor.
        p. cm. — (The Weekend crafter)
    ISBN 1-57990-336-3 (pbk.)
    1. Paper work.   I. Title.   II. Series.

    TT870 .T395 2002
    745.54—dc21

                                                    2002069440

10 9 8 7 6 5 4 3 2 1

First Edition

Published by Lark Books, a division of Sterling Publishing Co., Inc.
387 Park Avenue South, New York, N.Y. 10016

© 2003, Lark Books

Distributed in Canada by Sterling Publishing,
c/o Canadian Manda Group, One Atlantic Ave., Suite 105
Toronto, Ontario, Canada M6K 3E7

Distributed in the U.K. by Guild of Master Craftsman Publications Ltd., Castle
Place, 166 High Street, Lewes, East Sussex, England BN7 1XU
Tel: (+ 44) 1273 477374, Fax: (+ 44) 1273 478606, Email: pubs@thegmcgroup.com,
Web: www.gmcpublications.com

Distributed in Australia by Capricorn Link (Australia) Pty Ltd.,
P.O. Box 704, Windsor, NSW 2756 Australia

If you have questions or comments about this book, please contact:
Lark Books
67 Broadway
Asheville, NC 28801
(828) 253-0467
Printed in China

ISBN 1-57990-336-3

CONTENTS

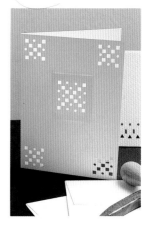

INTRODUCTION

DO YOU REMEMBER the first craft material you ever used? Chances are pretty good that you were handed a pencil and a piece of paper to draw on. And that piece of paper was figuratively given to you again and again when it was time to be "creative" throughout your school years. Recently I found a manilla envelope in my parents' attic filled with crayon drawings and a lovely get well card I made in the first grade for my mother. The texture and color of the paper were just as I remembered them: slightly grainy and a vague khaki color. The red construction-paper vase on the front of the card still held its vivid color, and the attempt at creating dimensional petals was still a success, even after years of being packed in an envelope.

Those early school experiences were formative, and some of us became inordinately fond of paper and its possibilities. I know I did. I was the creative type in school, volunteering to make posters for special events, dioramas from cardboard boxes, seasonal bulletin boards, and the requisite prom decorations. Familiarity with construction paper, poster board, and crepe paper was essential.

Paper is considered by many to be an ephemeral, if not disposable, medium. However, ancient scrolls of papyrus are still found on archeological digs and red paper flower vases in drawers and attics. For me, that's part of the charm of paper: you can create useful or frivolous things for today and save them for posterity. And let's not forget to mention the sensual charms of papers: their various textures, the spectrum of colors, and eye-engaging patterns.

The simple techniques you learned in school—how to paste, fold, tear, cut, and decorate papers—are a good foundation for your grown-up paper crafts. And you don't have to weld, own elaborate power tools, or invest in expensive (and sometimes messy) materials to create beautiful things.

The projects in this book run the gamut from a functional place mat to a purely decorative (and impratical) floorcloth. Thankfully you don't have to complete these paper projects in the space of an hour's classroom lesson. Take your time—what better way to spend a weekend! If the directions tell you to let the project dry overnight, put your feet up and have a cup of tea. Then start again the next day. And there are no prohibitions preventing you from working during the week if you choose. By the time you return to the work-a-day world on Monday, you'll have created something substantial from a piece (sometimes literally) of paper.

PAPER CRAFTING BASICS

Papers

Have you shopped for paper lately? If you haven't, you're in for a pleasant surprise. You aren't limited to creating objects crafted with grade-school construction papers or poster board these days. There's an infinite number of papers: from plain, stiff kraft boards to wildly patterned and colorful papers that mimic the pliability of soft, woven cloth. You'll find a wide variety of paper choices, not just in fine art supply and craft stores, but in home improvement stores, party and office supply stores, as well as from on-line suppliers.

ART PAPERS

A wide variety of fine papers are made for use with fine art techniques, such as drawing and sketching, painting, or printing. These papers are made in a variety of weights (thicknesses), with smooth or textured surfaces, and a range of colors. Use them in their natural state or embellished with whatever techniques you desire. The desk organizers on page 27 were made with a heavyweight paper artists use for printing etchings.

TISSUE PAPERS AND NAPKINS

Simple, white tissue paper has its everyday uses; green and red have their traditional holiday uses. Manufacturers also offer consumers stylish choices in a rainbow of solid colors that are paired with contemporary patterned tissue papers. You can also discover uses for the metallics, traditional patterns, faux prints, and lightly textured surfaces. Use them for decoupage (page 24) and as a decorative final layer for objects made of paper mache (page 56).

Decorative double-ply napkins can be used with decoupage techniques, too. You've no doubt seen the wide variety you can choose from in many stores. You can cut out individual motifs, use the broad colorful borders, or the entire napkin in a variety of ways. They make great translucent embellishments on a window treatment (page 15).

PAPER BOARDS

Single-face cardboard, sometimes called corrugated paper, is available in a variety of colors and flute sizes (the rippled layer attached to or between the outer flat layers). Your color palette is not limited to the natural light-brown color (called kraft). Today's choices range from pure whites to metallics and bold colors. Crafters like their texture and versatility. You can play with their surfaces to create a striking soft book cover (page 30), or combine them with other papers in collage (page 39).

Double-wall cardboard, the common brown cardboard box, is made of single-face cardboard with an additional face. It's the workhorse of paper crafting. Use it to form three-dimensional shapes to cover with paper mache (page 33) or as a substitute cutting surface if you don't wish to invest in a cutting mat.

Poster board (as every student and parent knows) is a useful single-ply board. It's lightweight, easily scored, inexpensive and readily available. Remember that midnight dash to complete the school project that's due tomorrow? Even grocery stores carry it. Manufacturers have responded to consumer tastes with fluorescent colors and metallic finishes, in addition to the traditional basic range of colors. Use it as a flat sheet or shape it into complex geometric shapes (page 42).

Illustration and mat boards are found in stores that stock fine art supplies. These strong, smooth-surfaced boards are available in a variety of thicknesses and colors. Store them flat at all times to prevent warping.

Foam-core board is made of two layers of smooth card stock laminated over a layer of polystyrene. White and black foam-core boards are commonly available in craft and office supply stores. You can't fold or crease this board, but it can be glued or pinned together to form three-dimensional shapes. It makes an excellent backing board for school projects and can give dimension to a flat project, such as a checkerboard (page 18).

VELLUM AND SCRAPBOOK PAPERS

Delicate, translucent sheets of vellum are popular crafting papers. They're somewhat stiff and hold a sharp crease when folded. Use them as accents in collages (page 39) or create whimsical shades for mini-lights (page 51). When you glue these papers, avoid using broad strokes of glue. Instead, apply tiny dots to prevent disfiguring glue stains and wrinkling.

Papers sold for scrapbook or memory album crafting are available in a mind-boggling profusion of patterns, finishes, and textures. To say they are infinitely useful and fun to use is stating the obvious. Their only limitation is that they are commonly available only in 12-inch-square (30.5 cm) sheets.

PRINTED PAPERS

Gift wrap papers, both coated and uncoated, are available in flat or folded sheets, as well as rolled lengths. Machine-printed patterns imitate calligraphy, intricate fabric patterns, and hand-blocked patterns. Japanese washi papers are printed with intricate patterns on fine-grained paper, and they're great to work with. Other handmade Asian papers are often decorated with clean-lined stencilled patterns or hand-printed patterns from hand-carved wood blocks.

HANDMADE PAPERS

Admit it: you may like paper, but you truly lust after handmade papers. If you have yet to discover the joys of handmade papers, prepare yourself. Their textures and patterns are alluringly seductive. True paper junkies hoard sheets of papers with names like *unryu, sunomi, hosho,* and *momiji.* Solid sheets formed with long, visible fibers and natural inclusions or sheets as delicate as handmade lace are just the tip of the handmade paper iceberg. Crisp sheets, thick, textured sheets, and even rolls of fabric-like paper delight the crafter's eye and touch. Be forewarned: they're a pleasure to work with and truly addictive. Use handmade papers to create a charming window treatment (page 54) or a decorative table accent (page 59).

Tools and Supplies

Most—but not all—of the tools and supplies needed for paper crafting you'll find you already have on hand. Tools like bone folders can be improvised with household items; cutting mats replaced with layers of recyled cardboard boxes. Don't feel that you have to run out and purchase a specific tool or supply item (unless, of course, you really feel you have to have one). Use your common sense and ingenuity to create what you're missing.

HANDY TOOLS

Metal-edge rulers are indispensable. The metal edge insures straight and accurate edges as you cut against them with sharp craft knives. You can also tear paper against the edge of the ruler to create a straight, softly torn appearance.

A bone folder is an excellent tool for creasing and scoring paper. If you don't happen to have a bone folder, the dull blade of a table knife is an acceptable substitute. In a pinch, your fingernail drawn across a folded line also will create a sharp crease.

Good quality drawing pencils and a small pencil sharpener should be in every crafter's tool box. A sharpened pencil marks a fine, well-defined line for cutting. Lightly penciled registration marks make it easy for you to place cut-paper motifs accurately on flat surfaces. A soft, kneaded eraser is also nice to have on hand.

A French curve and a compass are great for drawing fluid curved lines or creating circular shapes. In a pinch, use plates, drinking glasses, or saucers as templates to mark curves or circles.

Technically speaking, waxed paper is a material, but it's a useful tool as well. Use a sheet of waxed paper to protect glued surfaces when you press them with a weight.

Put your old textbooks or dictionary to good use as pressing tools. Glued surfaces dry with less wrinkling when weighted.

Keep a selection of brushes at hand for gluing, painting, and varnishing paper. A well-made glue brush with soft bristles is a wise investment. The flexible bristles make coating paper with an even coat of glue a snap. Take care of your brush and clean it in warm, soapy water after each and every use. A brush covered with dried glue is worthless. Period. Stencil brushes and other paintbrushes are valuable when working with paper.

Disposable latex gloves provide protection for your hands when you work with paper mache; unless you enjoy peeling a layer of dried glue from your fingers, you'll be wise to wear them.

Recycled materials such as food trays and plastic lids are excellent containers for glues, paints, and varnishes. Keep some on hand for a variety of crafting chores.

Pieces of soft cloth are also useful; use them to clean fingertips stained with glue and to wipe away excess glue from paper surfaces.

TAPES AND STAPLERS

Masking tapes in a variety of widths, types, and colors can always be put to good use by paper crafters. Black masking tape (purchased from an art supply store) has excellent adhesive qualities, in addition to having a decorative potential. Low-tack painting tapes, because they are less likely to mar paper surfaces, are a good choice when you wish to hold papers together temporarily. Good quality white artists' tape is a fine tape. Narrow, white drafting tape holds paper well and is not likely to mar paper surfaces. I like to use gummed paper tapes when constructing the basic structures for paper mache. Double-sided foam mounting tapes can be used to give layered papers dimension (page 45). Cellophane tapes, single and double-face, come in handy, too.

The common office stapler can be employed to affix photocopied templates to your craft paper. The staples prevent the templates from moving while you score or cut out shapes (page 42).

GLUES

Every crafter has a favorite glue. It's also safe to assume that every crafter has an assortment of glues stored away for a variety of uses. If you look around your house, you'll probably find that you have two or more types of glue. Examine your stockpile and read the labels to determine if they can be used with paper.

Polyvinyl acetate (PVA) is one of the best glues to use with paper. It dries clear, and quickly, and is relatively inexpensive. Simple white craft glue is a PVA glue, and the terms can be used interchangeably. You can dilute the glue with water to make it more spreadable or to use for paper mache. Other glues, such as wallpaper paste and rice-based glues, can be used as well.

Rubber cement is good when you need a temporary bond. A single coat of cement is repositionable. A more permanent bond can be created by coating both surfaces to be joined, letting the cement dry, then pressing the surfaces together. Spray adhesives work in much the same way. They're handy when you have large surface areas to bond (page 69). Be sure to cover your work area to protect it from overspray, and work in a well-ventilated room when you use spray adhesives.

Semisolid glue sticks, epoxy glues, and hot glue can be used with paper, too. You can use a hot glue gun and glue sticks to join together and construct dimensional shapes from cardboard or foam-core board. Don't attempt to use hot glue as you would PVA glue. You won't be happy with the results. That said, there are times when hot glue is just the thing. Decoupage mediums, acrylic varnishes, and acrylic mediums can also be used to adhere papers. They are available in matte, satin, and gloss finishes.

sizes, from small personal size cutters for trimming photos to the heavy-duty cutters found in copy shops and offices.

PIERCING TOOLS

The humble, hand-held office hole punch is not the only choice for piercing holes. Manufacturers have created inexpensive hand punches that can pierce holes in a variety of sizes and shapes. And a hole doesn't have to be round anymore: stars, squares, rectangles, and hearts (just to name a few) can be punched in paper (page 45). Eyelet punches make holes into which decorative and functional eyelets can be set (page 27). The throat depth of your punch is the only limitation for its use. A hole punch must be used around the edges of a sheet of paper. If you hanker for a hole in the center of a sheet of paper much wider than 2 inches (5 cm), you'll need to cut it out with a sharp craft knife or scissors.

CUTTING TOOLS

A utility knife with breakaway blades is an ideal tool for cutting heavy cardboard. Craft knives with disposable blades are a must-have when you work with papers and lightweight board. Change the blades frequently: a dull blade will leave a ragged edge when you try to cut with it.

Keep your favorite pair of scissors close at hand when you work with paper. I have a small, black-handled pair of scissors purchased in a photo store that I use only with paper. Woe to anyone who mistakenly tries to cut something else with those scissors! Handle scissors with sharp, curved blades and fine points with care. If they are treated like fine tools, their cost will be repaid over the years. There are many inexpensive scissors used for cutting decorative edges: wavy, deckled, or geometric. Pinking shears are well-made sewing scissors that create decorative edges.

Rotary cutters are packaged with circular blades made to cut straight-edged lines. They are useful when you need to make long, straight cuts. Manufacturers have created deckled and wavy-edged blades for rotary cutters.

A self-healing cutting mat is a necessity when using a craft knife, utility knife, or rotary cutter. If you don't have a self-healing mat, protect your work surface with a sheet of double-face cardboard or a thick magazine.

A paper cutter with a guillotine blade is great when you have to cut multiple sheets or many same-size pieces (page 48). You can find this type of cutter in a variety of

Techniques

DECOUPAGE

Decoupage, from the French verb *découper*, "to cut out," is the technique of cutting and pasting paper to a surface to create an image or pattern. Just about any type of surface can be used for decoupage: metal, glass, wood, cloth, and paper, too.

Simply adhere cut paper shapes to a clean surface with PVA glue diluted with a little water or with commercially available decoupage mediums. Make sure the cut paper is laid smoothly on the surface without wrinkling or creating air bubbles. A sharp, straight pin is useful for puncturing air bubbles, which can then be smoothed into place with your fingers or a soft cloth. A final protective coat of acrylic varnish is brushed onto the entire surface to protect the applied papers.

WEAVING

Paper is composed of plant fibers, so it's only natural that it be used as a material for weaving. For weaving at its simplest, cut slits in a sheet of paper and weave strips of paper over and under the slits. Use flat or folded strips of paper to form the warp (vertical strips) and weft (horizontal strips) to create the simple over-and-under pattern (or more complex patterns) of weaving.

FOLDING

One of the most useful properties of paper is that it can be folded to hold a sharp crease. On the other hand, a crease in paper is almost impossible to eliminate. That said, store your papers flat and be very sure you make a fold where you want it.

A single fold or crease will give a flat sheet just a hint of dimension. Combining multiple folds can create truly three-dimensional forms from a flat sheet. The Japanese art of origami is the most widely known technique for creating a three-dimensional form from a sheet of paper. Multiple folds can also be used to create simple forms that in turn can be joined to make sculptural shapes (page 42).

Folded paper can also be used to create other forms.

Simply folding strips of paper in half for weaving will give you a double-sided mat (page 65). Folding small strips of paper and interlocking them (page 48) present many possibilities.

STITCHING

Machine or hand stitching can be used to join sheets of paper much as you would fabric. Even more exciting are the possibilities for using stitchery as a decorative element with paper. Experiment with the variety of stitches you can create by hand or with a machine. Stitching is used to join sheets and embellish the Golden Temple Floor Cloth (page 71).

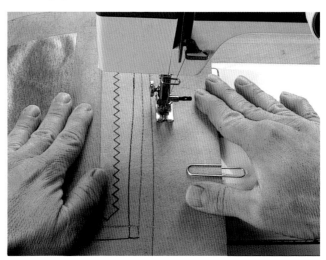

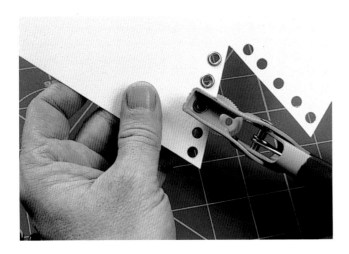

CUTTING AND PIERCING

Cutting a sheet of paper is not rocket science. You can make sharp, clean-edged straight cuts with scissors or a sharp knife drawn against a metal ruler. If you want a softer edge, tear the paper against a metal ruler or fold the paper and tear along the crease. Handmade papers and Oriental papers with long fibers can be cut with scissors, but they look best when torn.

When you want to cut out printed or traced shapes, first cut out the unwanted internal sections with a craft knife or sharp, pointed scissors. Then cut out the external edge of the shape. You'll find that you can make a smoother cut by moving the paper towards the scissor blades rather than pushing the scissors forward.

You can pierce (make holes in) paper with a variety of punches, needles, or awls. Holes can be functional (page 21) or decorative (page 45).

PAPER MACHE

Paper mache is the craft of modeling three-dimensional shapes with pasted, torn paper strips. Useful and decorative objects can be created from this humble material.

The paper mache projects in this book are constructed with double-wall cardboard bases. The bases always should be coated with lightly diluted PVA glue and allowed to dry. This seals the cardboard and prevents it from absorbing excessive amounts of moisture during construction. Other bases can be used to create paper mache objects: plates, bowls, modeling clay, or balloons. These bases should be coated with a thin layer of petroleum jelly before the paper mache mixture is applied to them.

Tear 1-inch-wide (2.5 cm) or smaller strips of newspaper; do not cut them with scissors. A torn edge exposes the fibers which helps to blend the edges when they are pressed into place. Dip a strip in a 1:1 mixture of PVA glue and water. Resist the urge to throw a handful of paper strips in the mixture to soak: they'll dissolve and you'll have a mess on your hands. Dip them, one at a time, until they are well coated with the mixture. Hold the strip over your container of PVA mixture and pull it between two fingers to remove excess liquid. Then apply the strip to your form.

Paper mache is a gleefully messy business—there's no getting around it. Cover your work area with plastic sheeting or plastic trash bags. Wear a pair of disposable latex gloves, unless you don't mind tediously scrubbing your hands and peeling off layers of dried PVA glue. Kids of all ages love this technique.

Rice Paper Blinds

Here's an easy way to transform white rice-paper blinds if you're the kind of person who likes a little color and pattern in your life. These blinds look great inside and out—light passing through the shades makes the colorful garden glow.

Tape measure

Rice paper blind

Decorative paper napkins*

Sharp scissors

Plastic sheeting or trash bags

Pencil

Decoupage medium

Small paintbrush

Stencil brush

* You can find these in craft stores, party supply stores, and gift shops.

1 Measure your window before you purchase a rice paper blind. There's nothing worse than getting home after a shopping trip and finding you've bought the wrong size blind (comforter, lamp shade, or rug!).

2 Use sharp scissors to cut out the design elements you wish to use. Set them aside. The decorative napkins have two or more layers. (You probably discovered this while you were cutting out the design elements.) Peel the printed layer away from the white layer.

3 Unroll your blind onto a large, flat surface covered with plastic sheeting. A dining table, or even the floor, makes an excellent working surface. Move any cords to the side; you don't want them in the way while you work. Arrange the design elements you've cut out. When you're pleased with the way they look, draw light, pencil marks on the shade around the elements to guide you when you glue them down. This is especially important if your pattern is a repeating pattern; not so important if it's a casual, unstructured arrangement.

5 Place the pattern element onto the shade. Use a stencil brush and a straight up-and-down pouncing motion to adhere the element to the shade. You may need to add a bit of medium around the edges of the pattern. Use a small brush to paint medium under the edges and a stencil brush to pounce them down. Allow the shade to dry flat overnight before replacing the cords and hanging it.

4 Pick up one shape and spread a thin coat of decoupage medium onto the shade in approximately the same size of shape you just picked up.

Stendahl's Checkerboard

Red and black are the classic colors for a checkerboard, but who's to say that you can't make one in the colors of your choice? Anyone for a game of checkers played on an apple green and citron board?

Black illustration board

Black foam-core board

Metal-edge ruler

Pencil

Utility or craft knife

Florentine script gift-wrap

Hand silk-screened kilim print paper from India

Rubber cement

Spray adhesive

Waxed paper

Heavy books

1-inch (2.5 cm) circular paper punch

24 unfinished wood craft circles, $1\frac{1}{2}$ inches (3.8 cm) or larger

Black acrylic paint

PVA glue

1 Measure and use a utility knife to cut out a 16-inch (40.6 cm) square of illustration board. Cut out a 15-inch (38.1 cm) square of foam core board. Cut out a second square of illustration board, measuring $18\frac{1}{2}$ inches (47 cm) square. Set the largest board and the foam core board to the side.

Using a metal-edge ruler and a sharp pencil, lightly draw a 1-inch-wide (2.5 cm) border around the edge of the 16-inch (40.6 cm) square. Then mark a grid of $1\frac{3}{4}$-inch (4.4 cm) squares in the center of the board, as shown. You will need 64 squares in all for the playing surface.

2 Measure and cut $1\frac{3}{4}$-inch (4.4 cm) squares of the Florentine script paper. You will need 32 in all. Measure and cut four 1 x 18-inch-wide (2.5 x 45.7 cm) strips of the kilim print paper. Lay two long strips at right angles to each other (a cutting mat marked with a grid helps you align them accurately). Cut a mitered corner with the craft knife and a metal-edge ruler. Lay another strip over the opposite end and cut another mitered corner. Miter all the corners and set them aside.

Cement together the largest board and the foam-core board. Then cement the playing surface onto the foam core. You may use spray adhesive if you wish. Cover the sandwiched playing board with waxed paper, weight it with books, and let it dry.

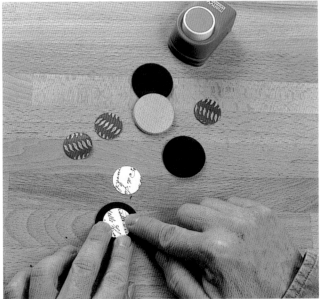

3 Spread a thin coat of rubber cement on the border strips. Then spread a thin coat of cement the border area. Let the cement dry. It's hard to reposition surfaces that are coated with dried rubber cement, so work carefully as you place each border on the board.

Coat the squares with cement, as shown. Then, coat each alternate square. Carefully position the squares on the board. Align the script right side up on four rows, then turn the board and position the remaining squares. Cover the board with waxed paper and weight it with books for an hour or so.

5 Use the circular paper punch to make 12 circles out of each of the two decorative papers. Set the circles aside. Paint both sides of the wooden craft circles with acrylic paint. Let each side dry before painting the opposite side. Use PVA glue to adhere the paper circles to the wooden circles.

4 Measure and cut four 3$\frac{1}{4}$-inch (8.2 cm) squares of the border paper. Mark and cut out four 2$\frac{1}{2}$-inch (6.4 cm) squares of the Florentine script paper. Cement the larger squares just inside the four corners of the large illustration board. Center and cement the squares of Florentine script paper in the border paper squares. Let them dry.

Not Your Grandmother's Quilt

This wall piece is a tribute to the thrifty quilt makers of the past. They recycled bits of outgrown or worn clothing and traded scraps of cloth to create beautiful quilts for practical purposes. This quilt has no practical purpose, but it's a striking decorative use of recycled materials just the same.

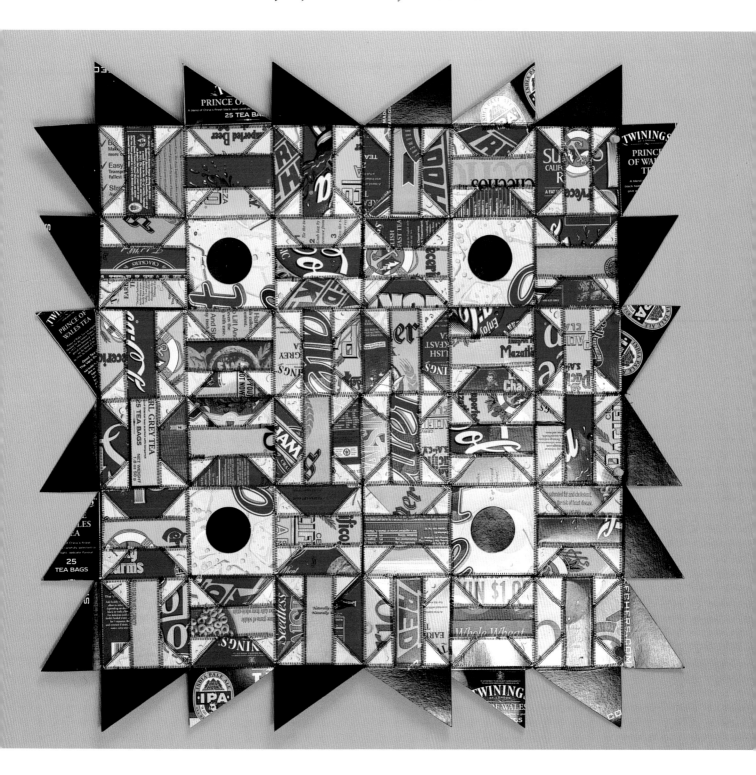

1 We used an adaptation of the Beggar Block pattern found in a 1931 edition of *101 Patchwork Patterns* by Ruby McKim. You can use the quilt block pattern on page 77 or consult any number of quilting books for pattern ideas of your own. Photocopy your quilt template patterns and mount them on thin cardboard with spray adhesive. Cut them out. Consult the pattern block illustration when you assemble your block.

2 Trace your pattern templates on the back of the cardboard. Doing so brings a bit of the unexpected into your pattern and the outlines are easier to follow when you cut. That's not to say that you can't choose to include a specific trademark or word if you so desire. Trace and cut out a few more pieces than your pattern calls for.

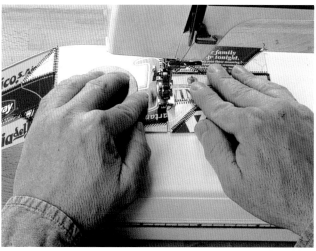

3 Assemble the smallest pattern pieces to create larger pieces first. In this case, two small triangles are attached to a rhombus to create a rectangle. Use short lengths of tape to join the pieces together on the back.

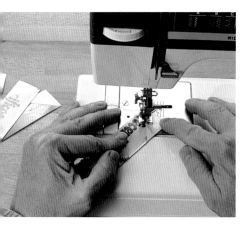

4 Join the small pieces with a decorative zig-zag or satin stitch on your sewing machine. Trim the loose thread ends with scissors.

6 Join three squares together to create a row. Then join three rows together to create a complete block. You can stop with just one block or assemble and join four blocks to create a wall piece similar to this project. The circle in the center of each block was created with a paper punch and adhered with glue.

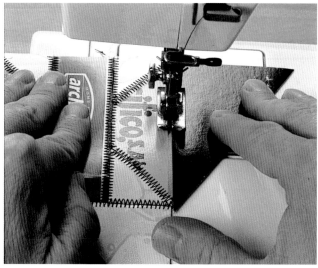

5 Assemble a square by taping together three rectangular units. Machine-stitch the units together after you have joined them with tape. Trim the thread ends.

7 If desired, machine-stitch a border of right-angle triangles to the hanging. You may choose to finish the back of the piece with a glued sheet of decorative paper. Eyelets are set into each corner of the quilt. Hang the quilt on the wall with small tacks.

Mad-for-Madras Photo Storage Boxes

Do you have stacks of vacation photos stuffed into shoe boxes (or worse)? If the decorative storage boxes you find in the stores don't suit your fancy or fit into your decorating scheme, create your own stylish boxes. These are so quick and foolproof that even the kids may want to join in the fun.

Photo storage boxes in a solid color

Colored and patterned tissue paper

Scissors or rotary cutter

Plastic sheeting or trash bag

Decoupage medium

Small brush

1 Cut the folded tissue papers into strips of varying widths. A rotary cutter used on a cutting mat makes quick work of creating more than enough strips. Set the strips aside.

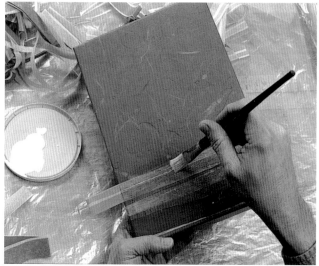

2 Cover your work surface with plastic. Start on the box lid by painting a wide line of decoupage medium across the width of its lid. Lay a strip of tissue on the medium. Paint medium onto the sides and the interior sides of the lid. Fold each end of the strip over the sides and onto the inside of the lid. Use your brush to smooth each strip as you work, pressing out air bubbles and wrinkles.

3 When you have laid strips across the width of the lid, repeat the process with strips running lengthwise. Use the brush to smooth each strip as you work.

5 Give the box and the lid a final coat of decoupage medium. Let them dry.

4 Though it isn't absolutely critical, matching the stripes of the plaid on the base of the box creates a nice touch. Start work on the sides, matching each tissue stripe with the one on the box lid. Use decoupage medium to attach a strip of tissue to each side. Overlap a small amount of each strip to the interior and bottom of the box. Then adhere lengthwise strips of tissue around the box.

Jute-Laced Desk Organizers

Simple materials and casual (but not sloppy) construction both aptly describe these organizers for the home office. Once you've mastered the construction steps it's easy to create different sizes and shapes to suit your storage needs.

140 lb. Fabriano murrillo paper*

Metal-edge ruler

Sharp pencil

Craft knife

Bone folder

Hole punch

Eyelets and eyelet punch

Jute

Cellophane tape (optional)

*Use any heavyweight paper you desire. Poster board and watercolor papers are excellent alternate choices.

1 Determine the size of your container base. Keep in mind that the base for your first container should be square. Use a 6-inch (15.2 cm) square base and 2½-inch-tall (6.4 cm) sides for your first container. Create a grid on your stiff paper using a metal-edge ruler and sharp pencil. Mark the height of the sides, then the width of the base, and finally the height again. Turn the paper and mark these measurements again. You will form a square grid of nine. Cut out the square grid with a craft knife.

2 How wide do you wish the top of your container to be? This will determine the angle of the sides. For your first container, make a mark 1 inch (2.5 cm) from each side at the top, as shown. Use a metal-edge ruler to connect the marks from the top to the corner of the base. Use a bone folder to score the lines of the square base.

3 Cut out the angled shapes you marked in step 2.

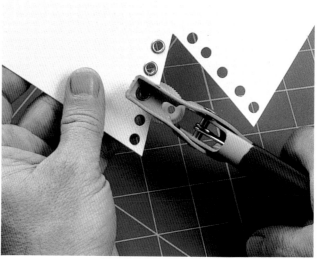

5 Use a handheld eyelet punch to set the eyelets along each side.

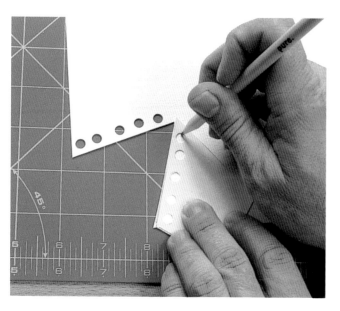

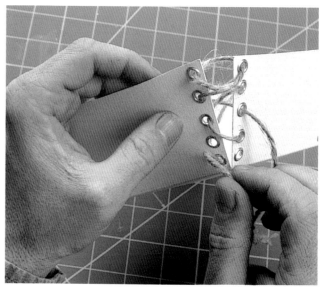

4 Use one of the cut-out shapes or another piece of paper to create a template for the spacing of the holes you will punch along each side. Use an odd number of holes. When you are satisfied with the spacing of the holes, use the template to mark each edge. This will ensure that the holes you punch are aligned with the holes on the adjacent edges. Punch the marked holes with a hole punch.

6 Cut four lengths of jute, each measuring four times the height of your sides. If you are lacing a tall shape, wind a bit of tape on each end of your jute to prevent raveling. Start lacing at the top of two adjacent sides. Bring the ends through the eyelets from the inside. Then cross the laces to opposite sides, just as you would when you lace your shoes. Pull the adjacent sides together gradually as your work your way to the base. End the lacing on the inside, knot the jute, and trim it closely. Lace all the sides this way.

Corrugated Marquetry Photo Album

Are you a tourist who enjoys using the panoramic function on

your camera? Unfortunately, those panoramic photos don't fit neatly into

storage boxes and usually don't fit in the family photo album either.

Here you'll use corrugated papers to create your own specially

made album for those oversize photos.

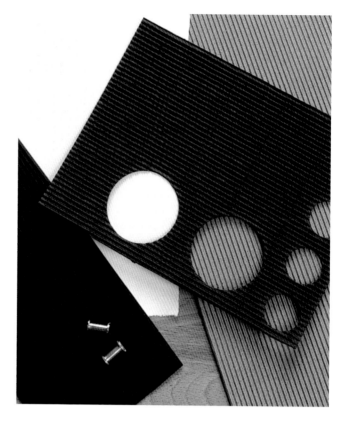

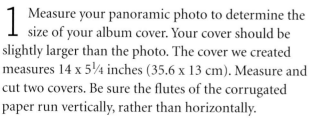

1 Measure your panoramic photo to determine the size of your album cover. Your cover should be slightly larger than the photo. The cover we created measures 14 x 5¼ inches (35.6 x 13 cm). Measure and cut two covers. Be sure the flutes of the corrugated paper run vertically, rather than horizontally.

2 Measure and cut the pages for your album. Our pages measure 14¾ x 5 inches (37.4 x 12.7 cm). Make a ¾-inch (1.9 cm) fold at one end of each page. The folded edge creates a spacer to allow the pages to lay flat when all the photos are mounted in the album. Set them aside.

3 Use a large paper punch to create circular negative shapes in your cover. Save the punched shapes for other projects. Use the same punch to create circular shapes in a different colored corrugated paper. The punched shapes will fit snugly into the negative shapes on your cover. If desired, use smaller punches to create shapes within shapes, as shown. Rotate the shapes so the corrugated lines contrast with the corrugated lines of the cover.

5 Use a small hole punch to make two holes in the front and back covers. Use the holes as templates to mark the pages. Punch holes in the marked pages. Use metal screw posts to assemble the album.

4 Measure and cut a piece of rice paper slightly smaller than your cover. Turn over your cover, repositioning the shapes as needed. Spread a light coat of PVA glue on the back of the cover and adhere the rice paper. Smooth the paper, cover it with waxed paper, and weight it with a book. Allow the glue to dry.

Thousand-and-One-Nights Vase

*Delicate Arabic script and stylized floral motifs make this
vase a stylish addition to any Scheherazade's decor.
Who knew paper mache could be so easy?*

YOU WILL NEED

Template on page 77

Double-wall corrugated cardboard*

Pencil

Utility knife

Metal-edge ruler

Paper tape

Newspaper

PVA glue

Flat container

Plastic sheeting or trash bag

Disposable latex gloves

Gesso or white acrylic paint

Paintbrush

Sandpaper (optional)

Scissors

Foreign language newspapers

Hand printed paper

Thai *unryu* paper

Gold paint or imitation gold leaf (optional)

Acrylic varnish

*Use flattened portions of recycled boxes.

1 Enlarge the vase template on page 77. To make your own template for a vase shape, make a rough sketch of the shape you wish to create on a piece of paper as tall as you would like your vase. Fold the paper in half down the length of the vase, and cut the shape with scissors to form a template. Trace around the template to make four cardboard shapes. Cut out the shapes with a utility knife. Measure the base of your vase shape. Measure and mark a square on cardboard equal to the width of the vase. Cut it out. Coat each side of the cardboard pieces with a lightly diluted mixture of PVA glue and water. Let the pieces dry for at least four hours.

2 Gently curl the vase shapes against the edge of your work surface from the top to bottom. Join the sides of the vase with short lengths of paper tape. Take your time as you join the sides of the vase. Tape the cardboard square to the bottom of the vase.

3 Cover the vase with a layer of newspaper strips dipped in a mixture of PVA diluted with water, as described on page 14. Add two additional layers. Let the layers dry overnight.

5 Cut headlines from the foreign language newspaper. Cut out the printed motifs from the hand-printed paper. Adhere the headlines and patterns to the vase with the diluted PVA mixture. Use a brush to smooth the papers on the vase surface. Work carefully to avoid air bubbles.

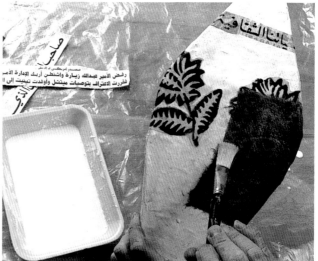

4 Brush the dried vase with two coats of gesso or white acrylic paint. When dry, lightly sand any rough places on the surface.

6 Tear hand-size shapes of the Thai *unryu* paper. Cover the surface of the vase with overlapping shapes of paper dipped in the diluted PVA mixture. Let the vase dry. Add gold highlights to the vase with paint or imitation gold leaf. Brush or spray the vase with a coat of acrylic varnish, if desired.

Faux Mosaic Wall Clock

Roughly torn paper tesserae (tiles) create a surface that mimics unglazed ceramic mosaic. But this mosaic is far easier and less messy to make. You won't need a large nail, either—the clock is light enough to hang on the wall by a pin!

Template on page 75

Pencil

Heavy textured papers

Colored pulp papers*

Metal-edge ruler

Cardboard cake round

PVA glue

Waxed paper

Clock works**

Awl or craft knife

*You can find these in craft stores that carry papermaking supplies.

**Available in craft and hardware stores.

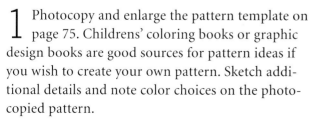

1 Photocopy and enlarge the pattern template on page 75. Childrens' coloring books or graphic design books are good sources for pattern ideas if you wish to create your own pattern. Sketch additional details and note color choices on the photocopied pattern.

2 Tear long strips of your papers, using a metal-edge ruler to help keep the strips a uniform width. Then tear the long strips into smaller 1-inch (2.5 cm) strips. Sort the short strips into piles of the same color. These are your mosaic "tiles."

3 It's helpful to arrange the small tiles on your pattern before you start. You can adjust their size if needed before you get involved in gluing them down.

Glue a background paper of your choice to the cardboard round. Trim it to fit. The background paper mimics the grout of traditional mosaic, so you just have to decide whether you want a light or dark colored "grout". Lightly sketch the central lines of your pattern onto the covered cardboard round.

5 Use an awl or craft knife to pierce a small hole in the center of the clock. Enlarge the hole as needed to accommodate the stem of your clockwork assembly. Follow the manufacturer's instructions for assembling the clockworks.

4 Adhere the paper tiles to the clock face with PVA glue. Leave a bit of the background paper exposed between tiles. Cover the entire surface with tiles, then cover the clock face with waxed paper and a heavy book. Allow the glued tiles to dry overnight.

Paper Quartet Collage Bottles

Admit it: Somehow you've saved up a pile of too-pretty-to-toss scraps that just don't appear to be useful. Here's an addictive little parlor game I like to play with them. Sort through your pile and pull out four (and only four!) papers. Then use those four papers to create small collages to embellish glass bottles, cards, scrapbooks, or even one-of-a-kind jewelry pieces. When you've used your first selections, choose four more, and play again.

1 Select four different papers from your pile of scraps. We've chosen corrugated paper in two colors, translucent tissue, and a hand-printed paper.

2 Cut a central piece of corrugated paper to cover one side of your bottle. Use a paper punch to create holes in the paper.

3 Cut or tear small pieces of tissue. Glue the pieces to the back side of the corrugated paper.

4 Embellish the front of the corrugated paper with small shapes of printed paper and scraps of corrugated paper. Use paper punches, decorative scissors, or tear the papers to make decorative elements for your collages.

5 Glue the collage to one side of the bottle. Cover the collage with waxed paper and weight it with a small book. Let the glue dry.

Star-Like, Star-Bright Night-Light

*We don't suggest trying to read by the light of this
striking lamp. Instead, use it to ward off the
wild things that go bump in the night.*

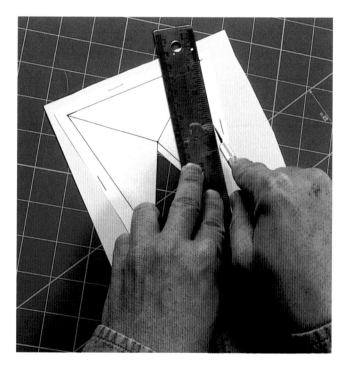

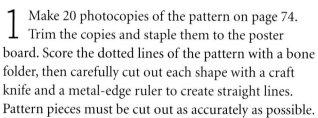

1 Make 20 photocopies of the pattern on page 74. Trim the copies and staple them to the poster board. Score the dotted lines of the pattern with a bone folder, then carefully cut out each shape with a craft knife and a metal-edge ruler to create straight lines. Pattern pieces must be cut out as accurately as possible.

2 Use a scrap piece of poster board to create a template for the placement of holes you'll punch in each portion of the pattern piece. The holes allow the light to shine through. Mark each piece and punch the holes. Set them aside.

3 Gently bend the scored lines to create a pyramid shape. Spread a thin coat of rubber cement on the flap and on the back edge of the adjacent triangle unit. Let the rubber cement dry. Fold the pattern to form a pyramid. Assemble all of the pyramids.

5 Join the groups of pyramids together with tape to form the starlike shape. You may remove one of the pyramids if you wish your star shape to sit flat on the table. Otherwise, don't tape the last two sides of the last pyramid together. Use a low-wattage single bulb or small strand of mini-lights to illuminate the star.

4 Work slowly and carefully to assemble the pyramids in groups of four. Use short lengths of tape to join them together. Pay attention, aligning the pyramids as precisely as possible. When you have them aligned, join them with longer lengths of tape.

Decorative Pierced Greeting Cards

The Victorians created intricate designs by pricking holes on paper items. The raised designs created texture on flat surfaces and allowed patterns of light to shine through as well. The modern crafter has a plethora of punches available to achieve similar, but contemporary, effects.

YOU WILL NEED

Scrap paper

Decorative hole punches

Sharp pencil

Blank greeting cards and envelope

Craft knife

Foam mounting strips

Translucent vellum (optional)

1 Experiment with your punches on a scrap piece of paper. Create designs that fit well in a corner and along the edges. Punches with simple, symmetrical shapes—circles, squares, rectangles, hearts and teardrops— are easy to work with. Note the depth of your punch and how it relates to other punches you are using, especially when you are combining different shapes.

2 When you are happy with your pattern, use the punches to create a template of the pattern on a scrap piece of paper. You can punch patterns freehand, but if you are making a set of cards, you'll find it easier to mark the pattern. That way, every card will look alike.

3 Position your pattern on the card and use a pencil to make lightly marked guides for your punches. Punch out your border.

4 If desired, you can create a central medallion with your pattern. Cut out a small square or rectangle from another card. Mark and punch your pattern on the piece of card.

5 You may simply mount the medallion on the card with small squares of foam mounting tape. Or, you can cut out a shape smaller than your medallion on the card and mount the medallion over the cut-out shape. This allows light to pass through the medallion. Another colorful variation can be created by backing the medallion with a scrap of translucent vellum before you mount it.

Washi Paper Bracelets

Use elegantly patterned washi *papers to make these striking bracelets. The construction technique consists of creating an interlocked chain of folded paper strips. Perhaps you've seen similar items made of folded cigarette packs and gum wrappers in antique shops and books on folk art. Often called "joint" or prison work, it was a popular, early twentieth-century folk craft.*

Washi paper or origami paper

Scissors or guillotine blade paper cutter

Bone folder

PVA glue (optional)

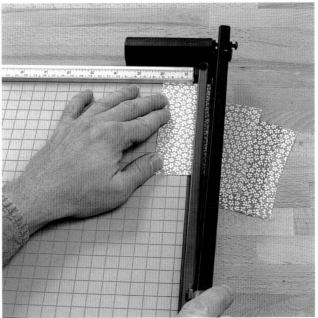

1 Measure and cut 2 x 4½-inch (5 x 11.4 cm) strips of paper. A paper cutter speeds up the task of accurately cutting the strips you'll need. An average-sized bracelet will be made up of 24 strips. Cut a few extra strips while you're at it.

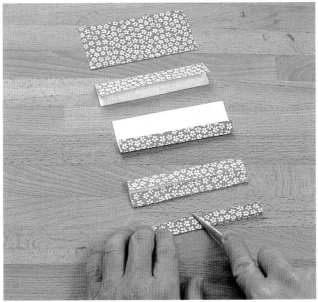

2 Fold a strip in half along the length, and crease the fold with the bone folder or your fingernail. Open up the strip, and fold the two long edges into the center crease. Fold this strip in half again lengthwise and crease it with the bone folder. Fold and crease as many strips as you think you will need.

3 Fold and crease the strip in half at the center. Open the folded strip, then fold in each of the two ends to the center. Fold the strip in half, as shown. Fold and crease all strips.

5 Continue interlocking strips until you have made a chain the length you will need in order to slip it over your wrist.

4 Take a minute to look carefully at a folded strip. You will see that one edge is a solid fold and the opposite edge is composed of two folded edges. Always look at the folded edges to determine where you are going to interlock a folded strip. Always insert your folded strips into the edge made of one solid fold. Begin by interlocking two strips at right angles to one another, as shown. Pull them together snugly.

6 Pick up one folded slip and unfold the ends. Insert the long ends into the first interlocked strip. Pull the chain together snugly. Take each end and fold them back over the first strip. Slip each end under the crossing strip. If desired, put a dot of PVA glue on the end before you slip it under.

Dreamy Garden Mini-Light Garland

Quickly transform a plain strand of mini-lights into a delicate floral garland. Festoon a wall in a child's bedroom, drape them over a gauzy bed canopy, or wind them onto tree branches for a midsummer's eve party. Translucent vellum and soft light are an unbeatable (and dreamy!) combination.

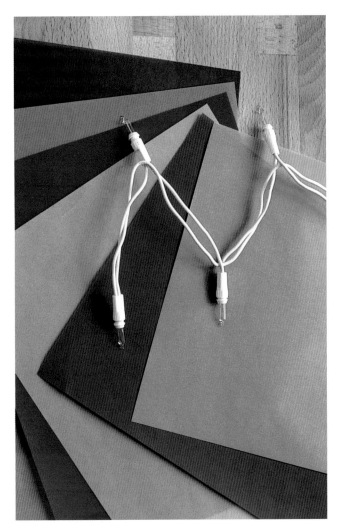

1 Photocopy the templates on page 76. Enlarge or reduce the templates as desired. Make several copies. Cut out the templates and arrange them to fill a sheet of plain photocopy paper. Use cellophane tape to hold them on the paper. Make photocopies of this sheet.

YOU WILL NEED

Templates on page 76

Cellophane tape

Translucent vellum

Scissors

Bone folder

Metal-edge ruler

Hole punch

Mini-light strand

2 Staple the photocopied sheet to a sheet of vellum. Score the dotted lines of each flower using a bone folder and metal-edge ruler. It is easier to do this before you cut out each flower. Then cut out the flowers.

3 Sharpen the creases in each flower with your fingers. The scored lines will show you where to crease.

5 Carefully remove a lightbulb from the mini-light strand. Slip one or two flower shapes onto the base of the bulb. Place the bulb back into the socket. The vellum flowers will be held between the outside rim of the socket and the base of the bulb. Fill the strand of mini-lights with alternating flower shapes and colors. Hang the garland of lights, and let the frivolities begin!

4 Use a hole punch to make the center hole of each flower.

Soft-as-a-Breeze Cafe Curtain

Catch a breeze with these simple old-fashioned cafe curtains made from an unexpected material. Decorative-edge scissors and hole punches are used to imitate delicate eyelet embroidery without putting in hours of tedious stitching.

YOU WILL NEED

Thai soft *unryu* paper*	Decorative paper punches
Sharp quilting pins	Curtain rod
Sewing machine	*You can special order this luscious paper by the yard from most suppliers of fine paper.
Sewing thread	
Decorative-edge scissors	

3 Slip the curtain panels onto the rod. Determine where the bottom edge of the curtains fall on the windowsill. Mark this edge with a crease. Remove the curtains and lay them flat on your work surface. Use decorative-edge scissors to finish the bottom edge of each panel. Trim the overlapped edge as well.

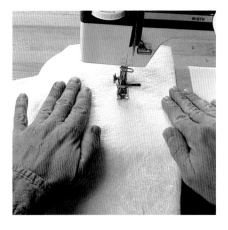

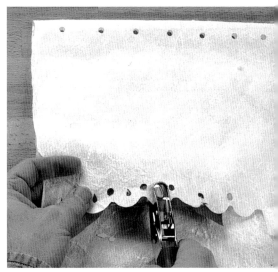

1 Measure the height and width of your window. Cut two lengths of soft *unryu*, each about 12 inches (30.5 cm) longer than the height of the window.

2 Fold over 10 inches (25.4 cm) of paper. Crease the fold. Use quilting pins to hold the folded-over paper in place. Sew a straight line of stitching approximately $2\frac{1}{4}$ inches (5.6 cm) from the fold. Then sew a second parallel line of stitching approximately $1\frac{3}{4}$ inches (4.4 cm) from the first line of stitching. This creates a channel for your curtain rod. Sew the second panel in the same way.

4 Remove the curtain panels from the rod. Use both handheld and larger paper punches to create faux embroidered eyelet along the edges of the curtains. You will find it easier to punch the paper if you back it with a sheet of stiffer paper as you punch. This is especially important if you are cutting shapes with large punches.

Caribbean Isles Frame

Random layers of pastels from the gentle color palette of the Caribbean islands evoke memories of sunny days, lush vegetation, and shimmering seas…even if you've only been there in your daydreams.

YOU WILL NEED

Double-wall cardboard*

Ruler

Pencil

Craft or utility knife

Hot glue gun and glue sticks

PVA glue

Newspaper

Gesso or white acrylic paint

Solid and colored tissue papers

Disposable latex gloves

Small paintbrush

Plastic sheeting or trash bag

Flat tray

*Use a recycled cardboard box.

1 Measure and mark two 9 x 11-inch (22.9 x 27.9 cm) rectangles on the cardboard. Cut them out with a craft knife. Mark a $5\frac{1}{2}$ x $3\frac{3}{4}$ -inch (14 x 10 cm) rectangle in the center of one of the rectangles. Cut it out to create an opening for your photograph. Measure and mark two $2\frac{1}{2}$ x 9-inch (6.4 x 22.9 cm) rectangles and one $2\frac{1}{2}$ x 6-inch (6.4 x 15.2 cm) rectangle. Cut them out with a craft knife. Arrange the small rectangles in a U-shape on the uncut rectangle, aligning the edges. Hot glue them to the rectangle. Brush all pieces with a coat of PVA glue that has been thinned with water. Let them dry for at least four hours.

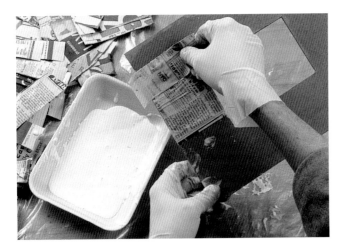

2 Tear newspaper into 1-inch-wide (2.5 cm) strips. Make a large pile of the strips. Pour PVA glue into a flat container. Thin the glue with an equal amount of water and mix it well. Cover your work area with plastic sheeting. Dip strips, one at a time, into the PVA mixture. Cover all sides and edges of both rectangles with two or three layers of newspaper strips. Let them dry flat overnight. Save any leftover PVA mixture in a covered container.

4 Use a brush to apply PVA mixture to a small area of the frame. Apply random strips or squares of tissue paper. Pat them down with the brush to smooth out wrinkles. Layer the different colors and patterns as desired. Give the frame a final coat of the PVA mixture and let it dry.

3 Paint both pieces with two coats of gesso or white acrylic paint. Let them dry in between coats. Tear your tissue paper into short 1-inch-wide (2.5 cm) strips. Dip strips of tissue into the reserved PVA mixture. Cover the outside edges and the edges of the picture opening with tissue. Let them dry. Hot glue the two rectangles together. Cover the edges of the frame with tissue, leaving the top opening free.

Mon-Kiri Table Runner

Creating family crests (mon-kiri) *is a centuries-old Japanese craft. The delicate, cut-out shapes—just a few of the many crest designs—are showcased on contrasting* unryu *and corrugated papers. Once you learn the fold, try designing your own family crest.*

YOU WILL NEED

Templates on page 74

Thin cardboard

Craft knife

Gold tissue paper or origami paper

Pencil

Sharp pointed scissors

Iron

Corrugated paper

Thai *unryu* papers in contrasting colors

PVA glue or spray adhesive

Waxed paper

Books

1 Photocopy the templates on page 74. The templates are sized for 5-inch (12.7 cm) squares of paper. Enlarge them 120 percent for 6-inch (15.2 cm) squares of paper. Glue the templates to thin cardboard and cut them out with a craft knife. Set them aside.

Cut out several 5-inch (12.7) squares of tissue paper and set them aside.

Bring one corner of a square to meet the opposite corner, as shown. Crease the diagonal fold.

2 Fold one point over at a 60° angle as shown in the photo. Bring the opposite point over and on top of the first.

3 Place a template on top of the folded paper. Align the interior edge of the template with the outside folded edge. Trace the design onto the paper. Cut out the design with sharp pointed scissors. Fold, trace, and cut designs as desired. Set them aside.

5 Measure and cut a length of corrugated paper for your table. Tear a second, slightly smaller piece of *unryu* paper and place it on top of the corrugated paper. Use small dots of glue to hold it in place. Glue the mon-kiri designs to squares of contrasting unryu paper and glue them into place. Cover the runner with waxed paper and weight it with books until the glue dries.

4 Carefully unfold a design. Press it flat with a warm iron.

Faithful Companion Silhouettes

*Could there be any more elegant way to capture Floyd's
(Fluffy's or Spot's) noble profile for posterity?*

YOU WILL NEED

Photograph of your pet's profile*

Pencil

Stapler

Black paper

Sharp craft knife

Sharp pointed scissors

Background paper

Frame

*Use your trusty camera or digital camera to create your
photograph.

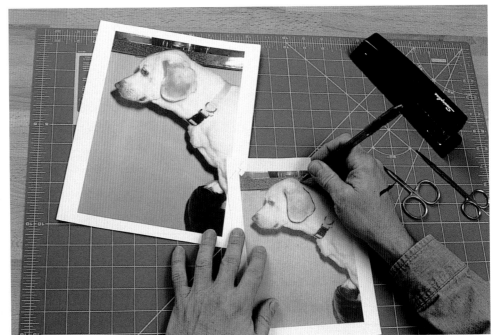

1 Fluffy may not take to posing at your command, so have your camera (digital or loaded with film) at hand. You'll never know when the mood may come upon her to elegantly crane her neck and turn her head...just so. If you're shooting digitally, you can enlarge and crop the photo with your computer's imaging program before you print it out. You'll need to photocopy and enlarge a film-based photograph to the size you wish.

Staple the photocopy or digital print to the black paper. Study the profile and outline it with pencil to define the lines, as shown. Outline any details (such as elegantly drooping ears) that you wish to stand out from the black profile.

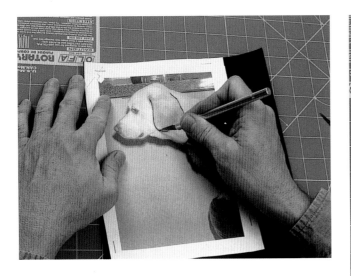

2 Cut along the outline of any interior detail with a very sharp craft knife. Make a second cutting line just a little bit away from the first cut. Use the tip of the knife to lift up the sliver of cut paper. If the cut doesn't show off that ear, then cut another sliver.

4 Adhere the silhouette to a bright colored, patterned, or neutral background paper. Mount the silhouette in a frame.

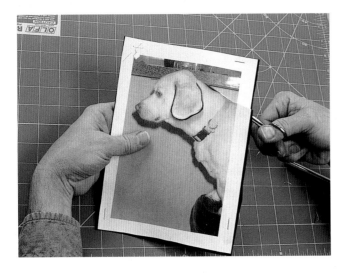

3 Use very sharp scissors to cut out the central profile. Move the paper, not the scissors, when you turn corners. (You'll get cleaner cut edges that way). Work slowly and carefully to capture the line of the profile.

Special Occasion Place Mat

Over, under; over, under. You remember the basics
of weaving, don't you? What could be simpler?
And what results you'll get when you weave
place mats for yourself, the whole family, or to
impress a swarm of dinner guests. Then pull out
all the stops and create napkin rings to match.

YOU WILL NEED

Hand-screened papers from India

Craft knife or scissors

Metal-edge ruler

Pencil

Bone folder

Drafting or masking tape

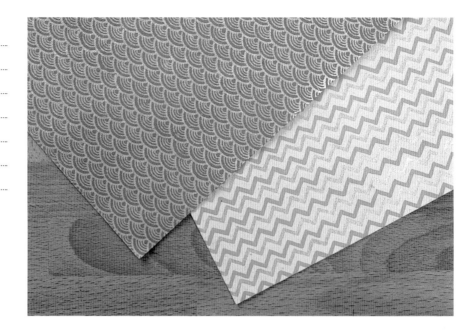

1 You can weave a place mat with just one type of paper, but using two complementary papers creates a more visually interesting weave. Measure and cut 1½-inch-wide (3.8 cm) strips of paper. You will need 21 strips that are 15 inches (38.1 cm) long and 16 strips that are 19 inches (48.3 cm) long. Fold all of your strips in half along their lengths. This gives your place mat a finished look on the reverse side. Crease each strip with a bone folder.

2 Create the warp with the 15-inch (38.1 cm) strips. Lay the strips on a flat work surface. Lay them close together but not touching. Secure them to the work surface with short lengths of tape. This prevents them from moving as you weave.

4 Fold the ends of the strips over and glue them down with a bit of PVA glue. Trim them as needed before you glue them. Turn over the mat, fold, and glue the ends as you did on the opposite side.

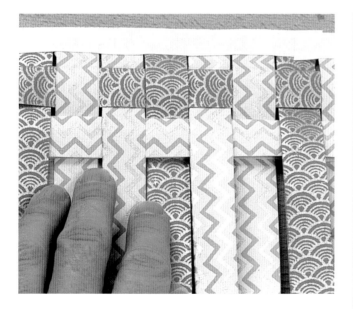

3 Weave the first row over and under each warp strip. Push it up close to, but not touching, the tape. Start the second row, weaving under and over. As you finish a row of weaving, push it up against the previous rows.

Weave all of the rows, pushing them tightly together as you work.

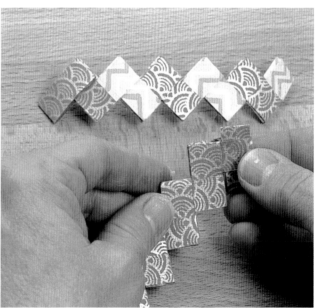

5 Create matching napkin rings with ½ x 4½ inch- (1.3 x 11.4 cm) strips of paper. Follow steps 3, 4, and 5 on page 50 to fold and link the strips.

Golden Temple Floorcloth

Definitely not a floorcloth for high traffic areas or muddy shoes.
But who cares? The dramatic impact this contemporary floorcloth has on
a room far outweighs its impracticality. Sometimes verve and elan
are all you want: Practicality be damned!

Brown kraft contractors' paper*

Oriental joss papers

PVA glue

Small brush

Napkin-size cloth

Waxed paper

Heavy books

Newspaper or plastic sheeting

Spray adhesive

Paper clips

Sewing machine

Various colors of sewing thread

Scissors

Acrylic sealer

*You'll find rolls of this paper in the flooring section of your local home improvement store. As an alternative, use brown kraft wrapping paper, but it isn't as durable as contractors' paper.

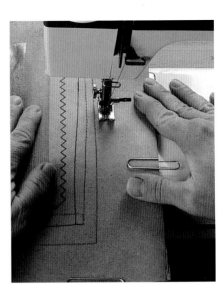

1 Decide how large a floorcloth you'd like to create. A 2 x 4-foot (60.9 cm x 1. 2 m) floorcloth is a manageable size to start with. A larger sized floorcloth can be created, but requires an extra set of hands and no small amount of contortion at the sewing machine (consider yourself forewarned). Measure and cut a length of contractors' paper to size. Lay it on a flat work surface (the floor is a good surface to work on). Arrange the joss papers in a pleasing pattern. Spread a coat of PVA glue on the back of one joss paper at a time. Place it on the contractors' paper and smooth out wrinkles with a small cloth. Adhere each of the papers, cover them with lengths of waxed paper, and weight them with books. Let them dry overnight.

2 Measure and cut four or five additional lengths of contractors' paper. Cover your work area with newspaper or plastic sheeting to protect it from overspray. Laminate the lengths together with light coats of spray adhesive.

4 Machine-stitch around the perimeter of the rug. Use a variety of stitches and colors of thread. The stitched lines need not be straight, and you may wish to cross over previously stitched lines in some places.

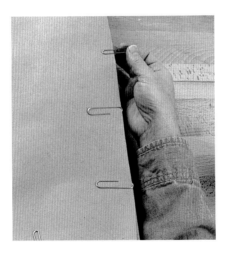

3 Spray a light coat of adhesive on the top sheet of the laminated stack. Carefully position the sheet decorated with joss paper on the stack. Hold the sheet in place with large paper clips.

5 If desired, spray a coat of clear acrylic finish on the completed floorcloth. Be sure you keep the rug safe from tiny (or adult-sized) muddy shoes!

Nesting Collage Trays

Once you've painted the trays, the collages can change whenever you like. Create a set of painted nesting trays and present them as a gift with an assortment of printed papers and a sharp pair of scissors.

YOU WILL NEED

Unfinished wooden craft trays

Sandpaper (optional)

Acrylic paints

Painting tape

Paintbrush

Gift wrap

Patterned tissue paper

Sheets of single-strength glass

1 Purchase one or more unfinished wood craft trays. Sand any rough surfaces if necessary. Give each tray two coats of acrylic paint. If you're in a hurry, use a spray paint. (Be sure to cover your work area to protect it from overspray). Let the trays dry overnight.

2 Use painting tape to create a grid on the surface of the tray. Paint the exposed squares with a contrasting color of acrylic paint. Let the paint dry. If you're in a hurry you can speed up the drying process by using your hair dryer to dry the paint. Apply an additional coat, if needed. Remove the painting tape when the paint is thoroughly dry.

3 Cut out central motifs from your patterned
papers. Tear small shapes of solid colors. Arrange
the shapes and cutout motifs on the squares.

5 Have sheets of single-strength glass cut to fit
your trays. Frame shops, glass shops, and home
improvement stores will cut the glass for you inex-
pensively. Cover the collages with the glass. Simply
remove the glass and the papers when you want to
change the collage.

4 You may use a bit of glue to adhere the shapes to
the tray if desired.

TEMPLATES

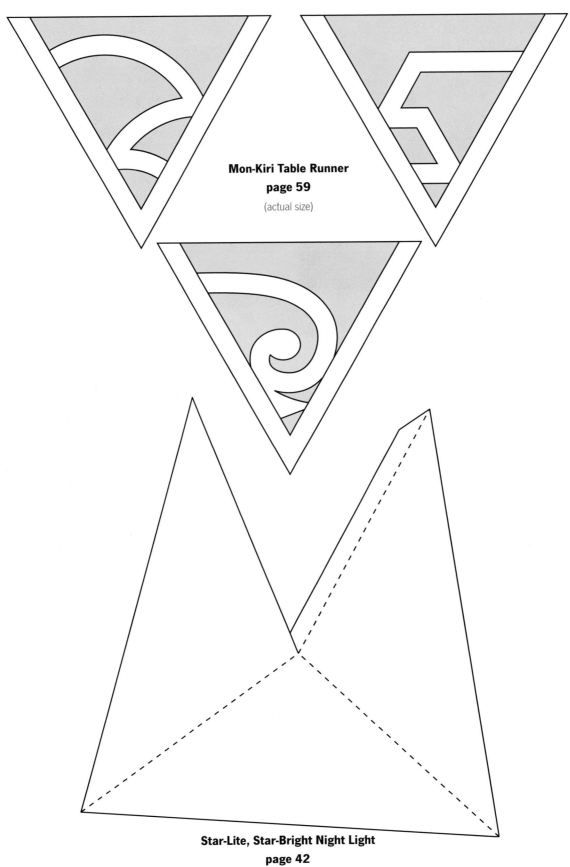

Mon-Kiri Table Runner
page 59

(actual size)

Star-Lite, Star-Bright Night Light
page 42

(actual size)

Faux Mosaic Wall Clock
page 36

(enlarge as desired)

Dreamy Garden Mini-light Garland
page 51

(actual size)

Not Your Grandmother's Quilt
page 22

(actual size)

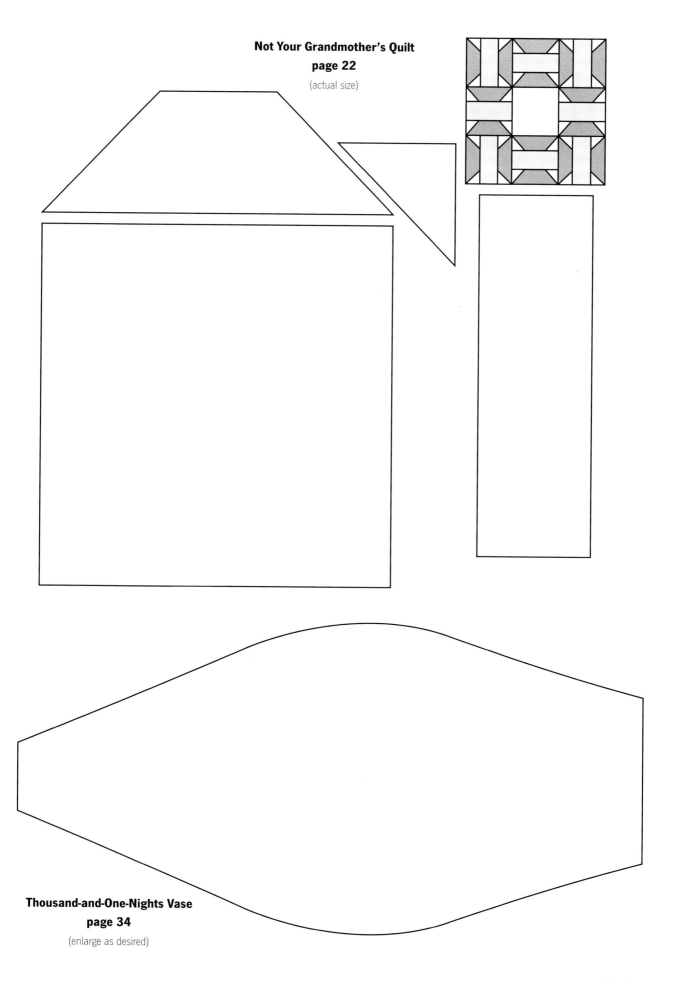

Thousand-and-One-Nights Vase
page 34

(enlarge as desired)

Denise Ortakales, *Klimt Kitty*, 1999. 20 x 15½ x 1½ inches (51 x 39.4 x 3.8 cm).
Paper sculpture. *Photo by Tim Cameron.*

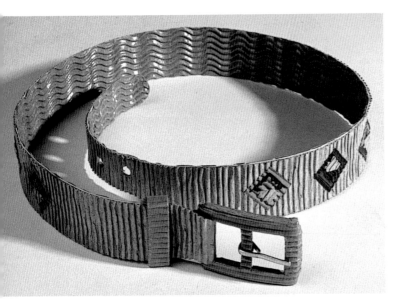

Linda Ragsdale, *It's a Cinch!*, 2001. 1½ x 38 inches (3.8 x 96.5 cm).
Mixed cardboards. *Photo by Evan Bracken.*

Dorothy McGuinness, *Cathedral*, 2001. 10 x 7 x 7 inches (25.4 x 17.8
x 17.8 cm). Watercolor paper, acrylics, and waxed linen. *Photo by artist.*

Karen Simmons, *Repose*, 2001. 16 x 4 x 9 inches (40.6 x 10.1 x 22.9 cm). Cast handmade paper with natural inclusions, honeysuckle vine, waxed linen, and dye. *Photo by Margot Geist.*

Katy DeMent, *Medicine Man Sconce*, 2000. 24 x 24 x 8 inches (61 x 61 x 20.3 cm). Handmade recylced paper, plant materials, wood, vintage postcard, and beeswax. *Photo by Bart Kasten.*

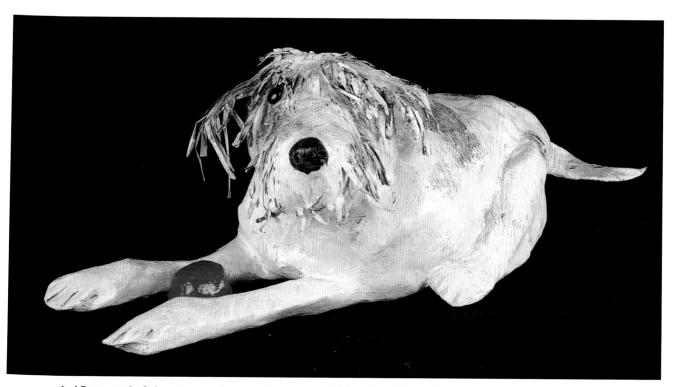

Jeri Rosenzweig Gale, *Miss Lucy*, 2001. 9 x 12 x 33 inches (22.9 x 30.5 x 83.2 cm). Paper mache and glass stones. *Photo by Roger Squires.*

GALLERY ARTISTS

Jeri R. Gale is a lifelong resident of Savannah, Georgia. Her business Very Jeri specializes in "pet-traits". Her household includes a son, two cats, and a fixer-upper dog. She's thrilled to make her living in a creative discipline that doesn't require wearing pantyhose.

Denise Ortakles is a freelance illustrator. Her work has appeared in magazines and children's books. You can view her work at sculptedpaper.com. She lives with her husband, two sons, and her cat in Laconia, New Hampshire.

Katy DeMent says her fascination with things from the past led to her work in collage and papermaking. She lives in Atlanta, Georgia, where she makes paper in a giant mixer and sometimes presses the paper under the wheels of her 1963 International Scout Jeep.

Karen Simmons, a self-taught weaver, began experimenting with papermaking in 1995. The handmade papers used to construct her vessels are made from plant materials gathered near her home in the mountains of Cedar Crest, New Mexico. Her work can also be seen on guild.com.

Dorothy McGuinness has been weaving baskets for 15 years. Inspired by the techniques of Japanese bamboo basketry, she has translated the techniques into weaving with watercolor papers. Her work has been included in *The Complete Book of Gourd Craft* (Lark, 1996). She lives in Seattle, Washington.

Linda Ragsdale is the author of *Creative Cardboard* (Lark, 2002). With her sister she runs Mixed Nuts, a light-hearted company that sells precut cardboard (naturally) furniture and accessories for crafters to assemble and decorate.

A NOTE ABOUT SUPPLIERS

Usually, the supplies you need for making the projects in Lark books can be found at your local craft supply store, discount mart, home improvement center, or retail shop relevant to the topic of the book. Occasionally, however, you may need to buy materials or tools from specialty suppliers. In order to provide you with the most up-to-date information, we have created a listing of suppliers on our Web site, which we update on a regular basis. Visit us at www.lark-books.com, click on "Craft Supply Sources," and then click on the relevant topic. You will find numerous companies listed with their web address and/or mailing address and phone number.

INDEX